This Book Belongs to Sophie Salmon &

Life that Starts on the Bed
of a Stream. She must travel
to Achieve her Dream.
A Small Silver fish with a massive
heart ♥ Growing & changing as her
Journey will start.
Sophie Salmon grown from a Parr
needs all her Strength to Swim So far.

All the Big Fish & Birds are A
DANGER . . . . using their
teeth & Beaks to catch her
Swim to the Sea
for plenty to eat
Passing the DANGERS
Sophie will meet.
Farmers chemicals
Polluting the river
Swim into that will
Damage her Forever.

...he water she needs to swim and progress, is taken by humans who ...ught to ...o thought for ... get passed. ...forward, but could be seals & Dolphins lying Sophie for Break

Sophie who has She will go the last. in waiting fast unless she's escaping.

ish Farms Ahead Providing meals
Don't seem to worry
.How Sophie
or she must Pass
be eaten
Alive. Swimming fast
so fast
under She'll dive.

feels

the virus,
the
Sea lice

The Disease,
thrive. Fatal to
who
Must

Salmon
survive.

At last out at sea. She rolls in the waves. Eating her fill is all she craves. Lots of her food is not there now. She

The Sand eels are missing, we know how. Taken to fertilise parts of the land. Sophie will suffer at the human hand.

HOME TO THE REDDS

Sophie will eat & develop into Beauty Packing on weight She's ready for duty. Return to her Birthplace will be a great deed. Back up the river so she can Breed. Salmon are precious, Salmon are rare, Sophie can do it, if only she dare

The Fisherman's nets to catch her
for dinner. Sophie gets passed &
into River. Dolphins & Seals are
the
As protected by using
thereBefore. the long arm of
Sophies protection
Law. Has to Be
Just
Or there Won't Be
Salmon for us to See.

On she will swim up ladders & weirs. Over the waterfalls without any fears. Passed all the Anglers who catch her for Sport. Sophie too clever to ever be caught. She looks for a Salmon with whom she can mate. A young male looking for his first date

THE REDDS

Avoiding the danger, Sophie Swims passed. Travelling upstream Amazingly fast. Reaching her Birth Place, We call them the Redds. Laying her eggs in gravel for beds. Sophie has made it & thanks to her Salmon will Survive for Another year.

Sophies Incredible Journey ends here. Lets all join together & give her a cheer! The Journey She took is what Salmon do. It is hardly surprising there are so few.

ABOUT THE AUTHOR

Ron Taylor retired years ago and now spends his spare time fly fishing. He is a qualified game angling instructor and fly fishing writer. Ron is passionate about conservation and encouraging others to feel the same way.

ABOUT THE ILLUSTRATOR

Fiona Evans is an experienced Derbyshire Artist and textile designer of 25 years who developed a passion for art when she was very young.

With a love of colour, patterns and photography, inspiration is taken from animals, architecture, travel, a love for the outdoors and interiors.

Bespoke original artwork available to order in pencil or acrylics.

Instagram @fionajaneprints

Contact: www.fionajaneprints.co.uk